DAPHNIS & RATBOY

for Aodh

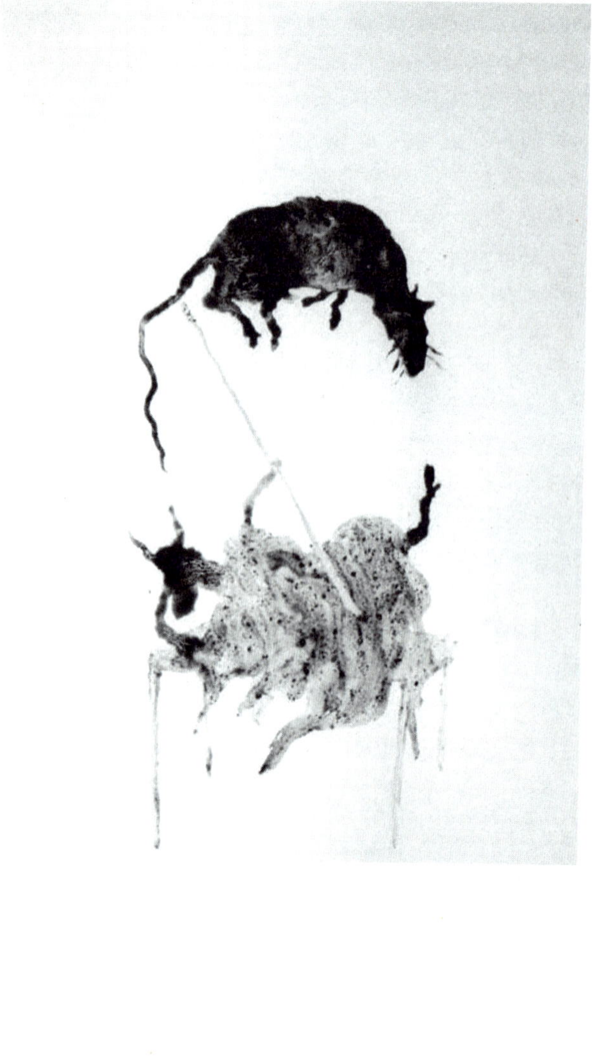

DAPHNIS & RATBOY

Jim Chapson

ARLEN HOUSE

Published in 2009 by
ARLEN HOUSE
an imprint of Arlen Publications Ltd
PO Box 222
Galway
Phone/Fax: 353 86 8207617
Email: arlenhouse@gmail.com

Distributed in North America by
SYRACUSE UNIVERSITY PRESS
621 Skytop Road, Suite 110
Syracuse, NY 13244–5290
Phone: 315–443–5534/Fax: 315–443–5545
Email: supress@syr.edu

ISBN 978–1–903631–57–7, paperback
ISBN 978–1–903631–95–9, hardback
(a signed, numbered limited edition is also available)

Typesetting ¦ Arlen House, Galway
Printing ¦ Betaprint, Dublin
Art work ¦ Kyle Fitzpatrick, Milwaukee
www.kylefitzpatrick.com

the arts council
an chomhairle ealaíon

CONTENTS

9 Eros Observed
10 Sun
11 Swimming
12 The Ugly Swan
13 In Woody Guthrie's America
14 Cattails, Water Lilies, Reeds
15 The Lost Coot
17 On the Lake
19 A Flotilla of Coots
21 Coots Differ
23 To Do Today
24 Wind
25 Oubliette
26 Drought
27 The Rosebush
28 Endangered Species
29 Song of the Epiphyte
30 Greatness
31 Watching
32 The Birthday of Ignatius of Antioch
33 Fog
34 Donkey
35 Magdalene
36 A Wasted Life
37 The Poet Hartnett
39 Daphnis & Ratboy
I Eclogue
II Paraklausithyron
III Puer Rattus
IV Idyll 1
Idyll 2
Idyll 3
V Haruspex
VI Pillow Talk

VII Post Script
57 A Poem for the Laureate
58 Hitch Your Wagon
59 Calling on the Master
60 The New Master
61 The Angel
62 Enewetok
63 Dormition
64 In the Temple of the Reformers
65 Seashell
66 Bishop Fisher's Tippet
67 Her Majesty's Education
69 The Volunteer
70 Days in the Playhouse
73 Birch
74 In the Cafés of Paris
75 The Promise
76 The Hypnotist
77 'That dog Patrick'
78 Lil
79 Narcissus Marsh
80 Baby Shower
81 Branchos
82 The Poet Ryan
83 10 Rue Lepsius
85 Daring Billy
86 A thought which had never occurred to them
87 Into the dark Midwest came the poet
88 Weather Report
89 Portraits in the Gulbenkian Museum, Lisbon
90 Heretics
91 The Day the World Ended
92 O Heart
93 Every Time
94 Remember
95 The Waterfall
96 About the Author
Acknowledgements

Daphnis & Ratboy

Eros Observed

On 14 February 1999 a NASA spacecraft began orbiting
the asteroid Eros, sending back pictures to Earth.

At last our rocket ship has given us
a chance to see what Eros is.
He measures up:
his skin is golden ('honey-coloured' NASA says),
and should we be surprised he's crooked, bent?
Of course he's incomplete,
or he'd have stayed at home, content,
instead of ranging hungrily through space.

And what about that skin?
Although it's golden, yes, or 'honey-coloured',
close-ups show it gouged and pocked.
But think of his affairs! So many
and so often violent – for countless years.
And yet a homely, pock-marked boy can find his way
into our hearts, and steal our judgment
and our wallet, too – more dangerous
than any smooth-cheeked rose.

O Eros you're exactly as we've always known you.
Still, it was considerate of NASA to remind us:
love is honey-coloured, pock-marked, bent.
And while this may have been a foolish and expensive
waste of soft-earned cash, if we could have
sensibly restrained ourselves it wouldn't be love.

Sun

Sun asked Water, Will you reflect my light?

Water said, Only if the sky's clear
and I'm feeling unruffled, but you
just go ahead and shine; it's not my concern.

If I stopped, Sun said, you'd freeze.

Not me, said Water, I'm free
in the clouds, I run in the rivers and streams.

Sun said the same to the creeping things
and the trees, Do you love me?

You ask too much, they replied, but
we don't mind if you shine all day,
so don't say we never did anything for you.

Sun went home over the horizon, thinking,
What's the point of burning myself up
for this crowd? So he rested,

and while he did so it was night.

Swimming

How strange after many years
to give oneself to the ocean,
touched all over at once
by intimate fluid caresses,
swimming with languid strokes
or frantically paddling
to catch a wave as it peaks,
riding the surge until it collapses,
spent, rolling in frothy spume
to the shore.
Comforting to know
one can still do it, but why
repeat the pleasures of youth
when they no longer please?
Maybe it's time for a new perspective,
reclining under a tree, watching
the swimmers play, tasting the salt
on the breeze; not the narrow
attention, the intense feeling,
exciting as that could be,
but taking it all in at once,
rain clouds sweeping the horizon,
scissor-tailed frigate birds
soaring above the shoreline,
breakers seething and sighing.

The Ugly Swan

Everyone's heard of the ugly duckling
scorned by the other ducks
until it grew up a noble and beautiful swan,
but no one speaks of the ugly swan.

At first the swans were tolerant,
but when it got older its ugliness
became an embarrassment.
And then it began to quack.

That was it for the swans.
We love you, they said, but you'd be better off
living with ducks. So the ugly swan, head drooping,
paddled off to a flock of mallards
who made fun of its swanish ways.

End of story. Through no fault of its own
the ugly swan lived out its days
and died without finding a home.

And that's why children everywhere
have heard of the ugly duckling,
but never learn the story of the ugly swan.

the tools to build our future
could be found in the general store:
a hammer, and a sickle.

Cattails, Water Lilies, Reeds

Cattails, water lilies, and reeds flourish in the
Milwaukee River
Before it reaches the tanneries downtown, and in
ditches alongside
The Chicago & North Western Railway passing
through the city.
Water lilies don't mind the shiny aluminum beer cans
bobbing
Among their flat green pads, and the draft of passing
freight
Cars lifts the fuzzy cattail seeds into the upper air
Which carries them east across the lake to Michigan or
west
Over Jefferson county (how small the farms look from
up here,
Green squares dotted with cows, ponds like puddles in
hoofprints).
Out of the shallow water primitive reeds rise up, their
roots
Grottoes for crayfish and frogs; not courageous like
oaks, reeds
Stay together, bend, each one perfect in its lack of
personality.

The Lost Coot

What's up
with this coot
alone
in the blustery lake
treading
white-capped waves –
miles
upon square miles
of wintry
dark green water
no other coot
in sight?

O coot
paddle & flap
a furrow
through
the turbulent chop –
break loose &
take off
for the rocky shore
the sheltered coves.

There you'll find coots
by the flock,
identical
sisters & brothers
flipping & diving
beak first
underwater,
grazing
the lake-weeds

chasing & squabbling
absurdly
as if the lake
wasn't big enough
for all of them.

Dear coots
it is
big enough
to lose yourselves in.

On the Lake

By these signs
you shall know them:

Indistinguishability:
a coot is a coot.

Irritability:
geese have their ways
and ducks make
very good ducks
but to the coot they are
interlopers.

Invisibility:
shades of grey against
the grey-green water
(hence the pejorative
nickname: mud hen).

Webster's New International (1929)
feels no compunction
in putting it plainly:
'They are stupid
fly slowly
and can hardly be classed
as game birds'.

So
when convivial
convocations of mallards
and Canada geese
honking & quacking
bring shotgun
toting gentlemen

coots
paddle oblivious
to their own
insignificance.

'Are those ducks, dad?'
asks the young hunter.
'No son. Don't
waste a shell on them.
They're nothing
but coots'.

A Flotilla of Coots

Our radars have detected
assembled in lake Michigan
a flotilla of coots
approaching the Milwaukee
Art Museum.

Their intent unknown
but chatter centers
on liberation
of art from the walls
ideologues from their ideologies.

The giant wings
of the Calatrava extension
have been deployed
in flapping mode
to frighten the coots
who have interpreted this
as a giant coot
promising assistance.

The loyalty
of the museum guards
(many of them
college students)
can't be counted on;
some have already
removed their clothing
and assumed
obscene postures
among the statuary
delighting
touring schoolchildren.

We are launching
a squadron of mallards
and Canada geese
to confront the coots
and discover their designs,

but this may be impossible
as the entire flotilla
has entered silence,
grouped in
amoeba-formation –
knobby feet
treading in place,
white beaks pointed
towards the museum.

It might be best
to surrender our arms,
legs, hearts,
and let the coots
have their way.

Given the state
of our country – divided
depressed
governed by venal,
delusional men –
rule by a flock
of coots
could only be welcomed.

Coots Differ

In this coots differ
from ducks and geese:
seeking their dinner
coots with a flip
dive underwater

while ducks tip
head-down, arse-up,
exposing themselves
to danger and shame.

When a coot wishes
to rise to the bright
noisy world it relaxes,
letting its buoyancy
bring it back up,
shedding its silvery
jacket of air,
rejoining its fellows.

So coots are happy,
at home in two worlds:
the everyday place
where they gather
and paddle, squabble
and mate,
and the obscure
solitary kingdom
of quiet, providing
sustenance.

They only despair
when they return
to the common world

and find themselves
next to some half-
assed goose
with its tail in the air.

To Do Today

Breathe 14,000 times, beat heart times 86,000.
Move among your fellow beings, compassionate,

envious, remembering your age and ugliness
(*ou sont les neiges* … etc.).

Earn your daily bread in frustration.
Fall in love *ad libitum*.

Remember those who have died
marked by the signs of life.

Look up.
Why are geese flying north in December?

Consider that no matter how bad things are
they will surely get worse.

Consider nursing homes
and the moral arguments against suicide.

Rest awhile in the incomprehensible.
'Think in your heart as easily as you can'.

Perform the evening ritual purification by water.
Renounce success. Solicit sleep.

Two weeks before she died, mother said
sighing, 'The things we do to keep going on'.

Wind

It wouldn't be bad being like the wind,
stirring things up, settling things down,
going nowhere, circling around.

The wind can't want to be anything
other than what it is
because it's hardly anything at all:

a tree bends, a newspaper flies by,
a coolness enters the day; 'it's the wind',
we say.

Everywhere it's different,
but it's really always the same,
whether it's whipping up flames somewhere
or bringing us buckets of rain.

It blows wherever it will
indifferent to praise or blame.

Oubliette

It was not for the enemies who had betrayed you
(no one would blame you for killing them off);
it was for the friends you had betrayed.

You simply dropped them into the oubliette,
a chamber hidden in the castle's stone foundations,
freeing yourself at once of fear and guilt,

though at night a wind from the woods
might bring a whimper
or a breeze from the fields a rotten smell
from which the imagination could assemble
a picture of something no one would ever see –

in a black pit, bones swarming with vermin –
impossible to forget.

Drought

Just as the economy was picking up
and people were beginning to feel comfortable
the drought began.

Everyone had pretty much everything they needed,
but as the wells dried up
they became irritable, reminding each other
that water was limited.

Those who had some left
began to hoard it, denying even to their friends
that they had any at all,
drinking in secret, rubbing their lips dry.

When it became clear at last that everyone was dying,
people began to weep –
only a few at first, but soon it was general
and as the earth soaked up the tears
the wells began to fill.

THE ROSEBUSH

puts out roots and leaves,
feels queasy,
develops swellings in the joints,

says to itself, be calm, hold fast,
resist,

but things get worse:
red tumors with a sickly smell
erupt from its limbs.

Cut them from me,
the rosebush says,
cure me of these unsightly growths.

Endangered Species

Its song established no boundaries,
attracted no mate

being mistaken for the sound of a lawnmower
or a dog barking,

so its future was certain:
extinction;

but those who have heard it say
that while the song itself was unremarkable

you could almost hear the emptiness
that came after it.

Song of the Epiphyte

We find support from other plants
but we don't live off them.

In temperate zones the lichen,
in the tropics orchids
and the staghorn fern adopt our rule.

Among rooted plants
we witness to the transitory

living our whole lives out on a limb
on whatever the wind brings.

Greatness

I saw greatness passing by
in walking shorts and pale blue shirt,
from the kitchen window
above the sink
as I washed the breakfast dishes.

It was the Master's biographer
Leon Edel
an elderly man
out for a stroll
in the morning cool.

I put the dishes in the rack to dry.
Greatness had passed me by.

WATCHING

What does the poet do at night
when his house is all in stillness?

He is listening to Beethoven
and watching the weather channel:
blues and reds swirl
over his daughter's house
hundreds of miles away – she sleeps
but her father is watching
the storm pass safely over her,
a glass of bourbon at his side
and in his lap a pair of pants –
he is repairing a seam in the crotch,
pulling the stitches carefully,
so as not to strain the cloth.
Contrary to common belief,
poets are simple people
and highly practical.

When the pants are finished
he will finish the bourbon,
go to bed, and let the world
he cares for care for him.

The Birthday of Ignatius of Antioch

From high up in the cheap seats
the men on the field looked like boys;
still, when the action started
it would be exciting,
but first we had to suffer a pathetic opening act –
a scrawny old Syrian heretic
sent to Rome as a gift to the Emperor.

It would have been fun if he'd run around
shrieking like they usually do,
but the leopards ignored him –
and who could blame them, nothing
but leathery skin on his dried up bones –
until the old man jogged towards them begging
them to act like the beasts they were,
and one of the leopards took a swipe at him,
ripping his guts out.

That was it: he died pretty quick;
the animals sniffed at the gore –
there wasn't much blood in him – and walked away.
While the slaves dragged the carcass off,
the crowd started booing,
so the trumpeters jumped up to herald the main event,
and the muscled gladiators marched in, glistening
with oil.

Fog

This, too, came towards me over the water:
a fog, spreading, taking breakwater, bridge,
yachts at their moorings.

If God is no longer the wrathful judge
before whom we quake, but a merciful one
who wants what is good for us,
still he is a judge.

In the fog bank even the outlines of things
had disappeared.

It is not easy for Mary to forgive those
who spit upon and torture her beloved son.

Only the ground was visible
at our feet in a circle around us; we debated
whether to go on, trusting our sense of direction,
or wait, hoping the fog might lift.

Some argued what mattered
was the intention of the heart; others felt
more was needed, an abasement.

That mercy will be shown to the merciful
seems fair enough; and for the others,
blessed are those who weep.

Donkey

It was a little past noon on a Friday,
the hottest part of the day,
and the donkey could find no shade
as it cropped the tough grass.

Then the sky darkened, earth groaned,
the donkey looked up and saw on a neighboring hill
three men raised above the others milling there.
The one in the middle looked familiar;
earlier that week (how could he forget?)
the donkey had been honored
as he had always known he should be –
crowds lined the streets offering branches
for him to eat, cooling him with fronds,
cheering him as he ambled into town.

The one in the middle had hitched a ride
on his back, and seemed to think the honors
were for him. He was wrong, of course,
but now it seemed he was being honored
as men honor one of their own –
lifting him up above the others, with a servant
at either side, in recognition of his qualities,
whatever they might be.

Magdalene

Naturally she was disappointed
to find the tomb empty,
for she had come to be once more
close to the beloved,
bringing her broken heart
to the threshold of the tomb.

Nothing could be worse
than this – an empty hole
in the rock, the shroud lying
on the ground, and the two angels
with their obtuse question,
Why are you weeping?

And then an ordinary man,
a gardener, appeared, handsome,
like he had been, and spoke
her name, and she understood
where it was that he had gone.

A Wasted Life

i.m. John Jordan

Full pint before him, silver hair swept back,
'Another wasted life', the teacher says
definitively of the dead poet

descended early under waves
of drink from which he sometimes rose
before being swept away again.

A wasted life pursuing love,
and alcohol which makes the heart
more wretched with desire.

The poet could not accommodate
the material world:
he choked to death on a ham roll.

'Another wasted life', the teacher says,
hawk face, glittering eyes, malice honed
by pub repartee and several didactic plays.

The Poet Hartnett

The poet in his later years expansive,
as vodka floated him over the poverty,
deceptive liaisons, marriage, unmarriage,
recriminations …

Navigating pub to pub the streets
of his adopted city,
hearing a joyful noise he follows
a crowd hurrying to where a parade
of rafts comes down the river:
they are his books!
A small venomous farm goes by
seething with lawsuits;
and then the Hag of Beare reclining,
opening her legs
to a queue of male virgins;
next a wounded otter, black hair
slicked down, flashing its sharp teeth,
swiveling a wary eye.

Lining the riverbanks, milk-skinned girls
shriek, scatter apple blossoms; old folks
weep to see their lives float by,
recognized, transformed;
and on the final raft the poet sees,
without surprise, himself,
waving, acknowledging applause,
his little eyes bright
as the silken river carries him out to sea.

DAPHNIS & RATBOY

I

Eclogue

Why waste the morning
waiting for a call
from the fickle Ratboy?

Do what makes you happy:
find a bench beneath a tree
and read the Eclogues.

A yellow finch flits
through the leaves
in search of berries;
red-winged blackbirds
peck in the grass;
swallows scoop up insects
over the water:

each according to its nature.

What's your nature, then?
To sit here pining,
or to withdraw
like the Shama Thrush:

'generally timid and out of sight';
'Their song is highly developed,
and their respiration determines
its rhythmic structure.
They are able to sing
during both inhalation
and exhalation'.

II

PARAKLAUSITHYRON

Is anyone there? Shall I keep knocking?
Try the doorknob? Maybe
he's sleeping; if it opens
I'll walk in softly, touch his shoulder –
eyelids flutter, a smile spreads,
he lifts his arms …

More likely he'll be humping
the girl from downstairs, or passed out
beside that pockmarked boy from work.

Should I knock louder?
No point if no one's there, and
if he's fucking he won't answer.

I ought to go – are the neighbors watching?
They'll get a good look
at a pathetic sight,
a timeless one – the aged suitor
spurned. Does the human race
never learn?

He's in there
slippery with sweat and love's
lubricating fluids, wrapped
in the soft limbs of the feminine.
Who'd want to lie beside
an old goat's dried up skin?

Not a sound. No one here. I'll go.
What's that? Voices? Laughter?
A soap opera from the neighbour's TV?

I'll wedge a note in the doorframe:
Ratboy –
I was here
– Daphnis.

III

Puer Rattus

Where is my sweetheart?
Is he in jail? Has he been murdered
by a pernicious ex-girlfriend?

At last he appears. Dark moons under his eyes.
He's met a girl; a pubic rash
all that remains of their sweaty fucking.

IV

IDYLL 1

ERIK
It's hot. I know a spot under a willow
where the Milwaukee river gurgles
against the bank exposing the tangled roots.
Shall we go there?

DAPHNIS
Yes, let's. I've a sad tale to tell:
Ratboy has bolted.

ERIK
Bolted? You mean he hasn't come round
for a day or two. Don't over-dramatize.

DAPHNIS
Two days? I wish! It's been a month.
He's dumped me, definitely. You're the same age;
can you explain it?

ERIK
Maybe he's sick or had to go home
to visit his parents. Why think the worst?

DAPHNIS
Because it's so.
I've heard he's out on the town
drinking and fucking like a maniac.

ERIK
So what did you do to turn him away from you?

DAPHNIS
Nothing at all.
He promised to see me before I left town.
Now I've been back two weeks and still no sign.

ERIK
He's straight you know;
he thinks you want his ass.

DAPHNIS
He's wiggled his ass all over town,
made out with Lacon, that pock-marked boy
who wears his hair in a mullet, and invited
the horny Comatas into his bed. I never
so much as touched him or asked.

ERIK
Maybe that's it – he wants to be courted.

DAPHNIS
So he can refuse. No thanks.
I've bought him a thousand lunches,
helped with his studies.
I think he wants to prove he's not my creature.

ERIK
You seem to think that being considerate
is all it takes, as if that's what we look for
in a lover. Polyphemus was a nice guy
with a cave full of grapes and cheese;
he couldn't see why the nymph Galatea
wouldn't fall for him – as if
she could overlook his single eye.
You're an old man; no fun
for a randy boy like him. Remember
the words of our Master Theocritus:

'keep aloof from the hurtful love of boys …
His time of flowering is spent
with his own friends, quite out of reach'.

DAPHNIS
True enough and truer daily.
But how does that explain two years of friendship?
I'll quote another Master back at you:
'They flee from me that sometime did me seek'.

ERIK
So, maybe it's time to return
to your first love.

DAPHNIS
Who's that?

ERIK
Your soul.

DAPHNIS
You're joking.

ERIK
Who comforts us when we suffer
a crushing hangover
or when the worried doctor probes us
looking grim? The soul's
the body's first and truest lover.

DAPHNIS
Good advice. In fact, I'd thought
my horny days were over.
Then Ratboy came along,
and set his cap at me. As Thomas à Kempis says,
'The devil never sleeps, and the flesh is not dead'.

ERIK
And as my grandmother said,
'There's no fool like an old fool'.
You're better off without him.

DAPHNIS
You're right. Guilty as charged;
he was nothing but trouble.
Under the willow here with you
I feel a quiet joy. Let's come here often.

IDYLL 2

ERIK
Daphnis, why so glum? Still moping
over the fickle Ratboy? Let's go
to the willow's shade; there you can tell me all.

DAPHNIS
OK, but even the tender willow won't help
me now. It's not the loss of Ratboy
that's got me down; it's what it means.

ERIK
Look! there on the path – a snake;
just a grass snake, harmless, now it's gone.
But what's that ahead? Half of something:
the hind legs of a rabbit, and an organ – a spleen?
Whatever the fox found not worth eating.

DAPHNIS
The way of the world: deceit, ambush –
grab what you want, and run.

ERIK
Here we are at the willow; there's
nothing savage here beside the river.

DAPHNIS
Nothing that we can see. Who knows
what's going on beneath the surface?
Ratboy seemed a loyal friend,
but all along his double heart was saying,
'I'll soon get rid of this old goose;
I've got all I want from him'.

ERIK
But maybe he wasn't deceptive; maybe
he was loyal, then he changed.

DAPHNIS
It comes to the same thing: no one
can be trusted; either they deceive by choice,
or they're unstable.

ERIK
'Our hearts are restless until they rest in thee'.

DAPHNIS
Well, that's a comfort – nothing to count on
in this restless world but fickleness, betrayal,
trickery. A little too Manichean for me.

ERIK
You're extrapolating from a single person –
a bad apple, maybe.

DAPHNIS
But if a bad apple looks the same
as a good one …

ERIK
Well, even the psalmist complains,
'This is what I fear, that the way of the most high
has changed …'

DAPHNIS
Is this a help?

ERIK
But he answers himself:
remember those times the Divine

showed faithfulness and power.
His absence is a sign of his presence.

DAPHNIS
So the only certainty is paradox –
endless and irrational.

IDYLL 3

ERIK
Daphnis, have you been to the river lately?
I was there today, it's lovely:
'The trees are in their autumn beauty
The woodland paths are dry …'
Let's take a walk there – soon enough
the river will be frozen.

DAPHNIS
It's been months since we escaped
the summer heat under the willow's shade.

ERIK
Then you were suffering Ratboy's betrayal.
I suppose you've learned your lesson now.

DAPHNIS
And that would be …?

ERIK
I didn't mean to be rude, but you admitted
you'd made a fool of yourself,
so I thought you'd given up these passions –
winter has its beauty, too.

DAPHNIS
I've learned a lesson alright, but not that one.
To give up love when you've been hurt,
brings no peace, and makes you bitter.
And to dismiss it as young man's game,
undignified for older men, disrespects the gift.

ERIK
But what's the point? You'll just repeat

what you've been through
and be sad and disillusioned once again.

DAPHNIS
Only the deluded can be disillusioned.
What I hope I've learned is equanimity.
As Job says, 'We accept the good things
from God; and should we not accept evil?'

ERIK
But is it worth the risk of being caught up
in desire, disappointment, and regret?

DAPHNIS
It's always possible that patience will give birth
to love without attachment, as Evagrius says.
Furthermore, love's gifts are worth the risk.
According to Callimachus,
'That old man ages more lightly whom boys love
and bring as their own father
by the hand all the way to his door'.
The holy spirit brings together youth and age,
making the young wise, and the wise young.
Or so we hope.

ERIK
In summer the leafy willow kept us cool;
now its naked branches let the sun through.

V

Haruspex

It's come to this – my hand
up a chicken's ass,
searching for the packet of giblets
that will reveal what's up
with the fickle Ratboy:
the gizzard's plump and firm,
the liver soft and bright,
but wait – what's this? – two hearts!

Liver and gizzards go into the stuffing,
the hearts into the roasting pan.

O Venus avenger of lovers,
as the two hearts blacken and shrivel
let Ratboy's double heart burn with betrayal.

VI

Pillow Talk

It's true he calls me different names:
'Lacon', he whispers, 'darling';
'Corydon, sweetheart'.

But I'm the one he's holding
in his arms – it's me he strokes
and rubs his face against,

so when he calls out 'Lycidas'
it's me he means, the faithful one.
Those others I suspect
aren't even real – one thing for sure,

I've never seen them here
where I wait all day long
for him to come to me
each night. He always does.

VII

Post Script

Corydon, is it true that Ratboy, yes,
our fresh-faced Ratboy,
quick with a quip, flashing a mischievous smile,

is now (so I've heard) a belligerent drunk,
avoided by people of sense
in all the riverwest bars?

A Poem for the Laureate

I was getting dinner ready,
figuring how to assemble the leftovers
into some kind of meal,
when I heard Billy Collins on the radio
reading a poem about American poets
looking out the window at a bird, a taxi,
'a limb knocked down by the wind'.
I paused – looking at the squash, the fava beans –
because I, too, am willing to find meaning,
however trivial, in the mundane,

and when the poem ended with a shift in image,
a spurious reach for significance –
'a woman's heart of stone',
that's just shit, I would have said
if anyone had asked me what I thought of it,
just plain shit,
but nobody had, so I said it anyway.

Hitch Your Wagon

'When I found a younger poet whom I admired,
I tried to push the poet –
publications, awards, fellowships –
to call other people's attention to the poetry'.

– Donald Hall

Calling On the Master

The Master has invited you to call on him.
The address takes you to a street
of brick apartment buildings where you follow
the gold-leafed numbers on the transoms.

You had gotten off the bus several blocks before
to prepare yourself, but even then you knew
you'd never ring the bell, and knowing this
had given you the courage to come this far.

Stopping at one building like the others,
windows glowing in the dusk, you know
you will do nothing to change your life.

You look at the address written on a slip of paper,
then at the gold-leafed numbers on the glass.

The New Master

Word went out – a master had arrived,
not the cookie-cutter foreign swami badgering
stoned youth on sexual abstinence and sobriety,
but one like us with a new teaching.

A house in the city: dim lights, a large room,
fifty people packed together
sitting on the floor, whispers, nervous laughter.

The master appeared in the doorway,
about thirty, bearded, in levis and flannel shirt.

A young man spoke courageously
for everyone, 'So, what do you have to tell us?
What's your message?' The master replied,
'You're talking through your cunt!'

Silence followed, then the sound of people
getting up and leaving. Everyone agreed
this was not the master they were looking for.

had nothing against the body he'd been given,
and was willing to try it out as a way to love,
but found it awkward with its angles and densities
for one who remembered still the angelic way:

Easier then Air with Air, if Spirits embrace
Total they mix Union of Pure with Pure
Desiring …

As years went by, he wondered if this recollection
was the dream that humans have, a fantasy
born of disgust with the flesh, and fear of death.

And so he learned to love as mortals did –
desire, disappointment and remorse.

Sometimes he wondered if he'd ever felt
the ecstasy his body now denied him, and what
his mission was for which this body was required:
something to do, perhaps, with learning sorrow.

Enewetok

He was the mysterious uncle who appeared
at the door – 'Eh, mama stay?' –
tanned dark as a native, speaking pidgin English,
a stranger my sister and I were afraid to let in.
'You no remembah your uncle Harold?'

Back from a construction job
at the nuclear proving grounds on Enewetok,
he brought us a box of seashells
slipped past the Geiger counter at the airport.

It was 1952;
we were building a carapace of weaponry.

My father let us keep the shells in the garage
where I held the speckled cowries and cones,
the flesh-pink conches, uneasily aware
they might hold invisible poisons that could kill us all.

Dormition

When Mary slept, her son
lifted her soul in swaddling clothes
as she once lifted him
to show the wise their journey
hadn't been in vain,
when in the sweet warmth of the barn
the child joined the family
of humans and domesticated animals.

How much it hurt her when she stood
helpless to protect him as he died
in agony, but 'all our mothers bear us
for pain and for death', as Julian says.

When her time came, she found
his death had taken pain
away from death – she fell asleep
and he became her mother,
bearing her in joy, lifting her
for all the wise to see and understand
that he will do for us
all that we wish to do but are unable to.

In the Temple of the Reformers

In the temple of the reformers I saw
how much they'd improved our religion:
spare but costly furnishings
shone quietly; choristers entered singing
an ancient hymn, one of ours,
more tastefully than we'd have done.

Here were no images, so strong was their faith;
they recognized God's human form,
but saw this as a phase,
his gruesome death unhealthy to dwell upon.

I partook of the sacred offerings –
the cool sweet wine, the wholewheat loaf –
and returned to my place, chewing.

They had improved our religion
as befits a people accustomed to rule,
comfortable with power, at ease with certainty.
But it is not for us whose faith is weak.

Idols prop us up on every side.
We need a human God who failed
and still was God. We need to see
his bleeding wounds, his agony;
we need to see him dead in his mother's arms.

We are not worthy of their deity.
We need (it shames me to say it – nothing
more reveals our savagery), we need to
eat God's flesh and drink God's blood.

Seashell

A shell in a glass case, genus conus,
unremarkable but for the exposure
of the underlying nacre, the lustrous 'mother of pearl',
where the brown outer layer has been worn away
by hands worrying it.

A card says it belonged once to Sir Thomas Wyatt.
Imagine it in his hands as he considered
that the woman who had been his mistress was now
  wife
to the paranoid, bloodthirsty Henry VIII.

Bishop Fisher's Tippet

When the lieutenant entered Fisher's cell
to tell the bishop it would soon be time
for his beheading,

Fisher asked to take a nap,
for he had not slept well that night
owing to illness.

Later when he woke and dressed
he asked for his furred tippet,
to protect his health against the cold
in the last half-hour of his life.

And when the bishop's head
was placed on London Bridge
it seemed to speak.

No record's left
of what it said, but at the end
this was John Fisher's message:

Pity, mercy, equity and justice
have no honour in the counsels of a king;
when you are weary take a nap –
you'll feel better for it;
and a furred tippet on a cold morning
is a great comfort.

So the executioner
threw the head into the river
and replaced it with the head of Thomas More.

But that head, too,
brought the king no peace.

Her Majesty's Education

'Glimpse inside Royal family's private world'
– Andrew Pierce, *The Daily Telegraph*, 3 July 2008, p. 13.

I

'Let us eat outdoors', said, the Queen Mother
to her butler, 'for my birthday lunch'.

Under the trees a table was laid with the usual
gold and silver plate, heirloom china, ornate cutlery,
and the heavily scented flower arrangements
favoured by the Queen Mother.

Heidsieck sparkled in the flutes
as the Royal family and their most trusted courtiers,
relaxed and at ease in the privacy of Clarence House,
the Queen Mother's beloved London home, grew spirited.

'Bring us a rifle, Billy', said the Queen Mother to her butler;
'between courses we'll have a go at the squirrels!'
'It might cause annoyance to your neighbors, ma'am',
replied her private secretary.

Through experiences such as this
her Majesty the Queen
grew sensitive to the responsibilities of her station.

II

When the 'people's princess' died, the Queen
was advised to go out among the people
to show she too had the common touch.
Taken to a little shop, her attention
was attracted by a stack of brightly coloured bowls.

'Whatever are they made of?' she marvelled.
'They're plastic, ma'am', said the shopkeeper
to the Queen who had never seen the like of it before.

Volunteer

A green shoot among the chrysanthemums:

'volunteers' they're called –
a seed blew in and settled.

Pluck it out before it roots itself;
the unexpected visitor is always trouble.

Or let it grow to see what it becomes
or rather is.

Most likely, though, after its
first enthusiastic growth

you'll find one day it's gone,
just when you imagined

it might become your darling.

Days in the Playhouse

I sought love out
where it could be found:
in bars on Bourbon
and Decatur Streets
with little Dennis,
Donny, Ron,
Minnesota Scott,
and Johnny C.

Bruce Springsteen played
on the phonograph
above the bed
in slave quarters
where Johnny lived.
We rocked and rolled
in tropic heat
until worn out
we fell asleep.
When I woke up
he'd gone and left
a note which said
'I'm not much good
at mournings' (sic).
I took my throbbing
headache home;
if this was love
I'd had enough.
But two weeks later
in the bar
he handed me
a napkin folded:

'Spend the night
with me', it said
in red ballpoint.
'OK', I said.

Days in the Playhouse
with Eddy the barker,
Jimmy Maloney
the union goon
with a .38
in a paper bag,
Wayne the waiter,
the con man Dux.
We couldn't believe
there was anything else
for us but hope
that somehow
love would find us
waiting on barstools
drinking and listening
to juke box hits:
'Voulez-vous couchez
avec moi, ce soir?';
'Why don't we get drunk
and screw'.

Those days are gone
like mist, like fog;
Jimmy was murdered,
Johnny left town,
Dux disappeared.
But nothing is ever
erased from our lives:
Ivy puts a bottle
of whisky on the bar
saying, 'Help yourself,

love'; Bobby is pouring me
tumblers of brandy;
Johnny and I
pose for a photo
standing together
not quite arm in arm
in front of the last
Desire streetcar
behind the Café du Monde.

Birch

Not like the willow will it bow to us
nor like the fir tree bend its boughs.

A cloak of leaves around its shoulders
sets off the gleaming whiteness of its trunk.

A delight to the eyes
its gracefulness, though it provides

the weary traveller neither the elm's
restful shade, nor the pine's soft, fragrant bed.

In the Cafés of Paris

After dangerous trips on horseback
into the desert,
following the routes of slave caravans,
trading guns for coffee, animal skins, ivory,

suffering adversity to master it
as he always had – prize-winning schoolboy,
feral teenage poet –

taking pleasure in nothing
but the discovery everywhere of ignorance
which justified a superiority
to which he felt uniquely entitled,

he died raving, frantic to escape
the world he was at last already leaving,

while in the cafés of Paris young poets
traded rumors of his imminent return
to assume his place in the pantheon of their hearts
and the pages of their literary magazines.

The Promise

as light recedes in the west
a thinnest sliver of moon

in spite of everything
the promised hope

waxing or waning

even when obscured by clouds

The Hypnotist

fit the part – black coat and beard,
mellifluous voice. Volunteers
came up wooden steps from the auditorium,

eager for something new
at the risk of humiliation, and one
determined to prove he couldn't be taken in.

Soon they all were arranged
in postures of catatonia. Pushed gently
they fell like boards face down to the floor,
caught by an assistant at the last moment.

As a bonus, and to prove hypnosis
neither insidious nor a parlor trick,
one who wanted to quit smoking was told
he'd feel sick when he reached for a cigarette.

Post-hypnotic suggestion. Imagine
feeling hungry when you smelled a steak, anger
when humiliated, desire for every pretty face.

'THAT DOG PATRICK',

Swift wrote Stella, 'is abroad, and drinking,
and I can't get my nightgown'.
But when Patrick 'the extravagant whelp,
had a fire ready' for his master's return,
Swift 'pickt off the coals' before going to bed.

Stella and Mrs. Dingley understood
how maddening these people could be
among whom they lived, had grown fond of
against their wills, and even come to resemble

as they resigned themselves to residence
'in a most obscure disagreeable country',
contributing to the national character their own
eccentricities which they labeled 'reason'.

Lil

Enjoying a cup of tea, a bit of bread
slathered with jam, Lil sat in the kitchen
as long as she could, before pushing the hoover
over the carpets quickly with one hand,
a cigarette in the other trailing ash.

Her children grown and grown away,
a husband, 'him', with whom she didn't talk,
curiosity about the village and countryside
her vocation.

After an absence she appeared one morning
to quit her weekly cleaning job –
round red cheeks now yellow and sunken,
but the smile still bright – beaming,
with the usual upbeat singsong, saying,
'I've got cancer!' as if she'd won the lottery.

NARCISSUS MARSH,

Bishop of Ferns and Leighlin,
Archbishop of Cashel, Dublin, and Armagh,
Provost of Trinity College,
was sadly disappointed his residence
in Staplestown provided few subjects
worthy of study for his projected
'history of the generation of insects ...,
and especially of flies the fewest
that I ever saw in any place
and of those not one rare or unusual'.

Building Ireland's first public library,
a new chapel at Trinity College,
and a larger residence hall for 340
young scholars who wearied him
for 'they are both rude and ignorant'
brought small pleasure; even his experiments
with magnets for the Dublin
Philosophical Society were no substitute
for the fame he would have enjoyed
had he been favored to live in a bog
thick with unusual flies.

Baby Shower

In the middle of the room sat a young woman
with what seemed a soccer ball in her stomach
surrounded by a swarm of women
bearing gifts; on the fringe a few irrelevant males
hovered, confused.

I kept looking out the window,
waiting for the shower of babies to fall,
covering the grass like the first snowfall did
a few days earlier, and the red and yellow leaves
before that, but I never saw them.
Maybe it's like Peter Pan –
you have to believe.

What I saw was platters of raw vegetables,
a bucket of iced coke –
this is what the females lived on;
some of the drones sipped vodka from coffee mugs.

A few months earlier
the pregnant woman had given birth to a dead baby.
Maybe that was the baby shower,
and all this humming and buzzing was something else –
telling the new baby what a wonderful loving world
was waiting for it, to hold on
just a couple months more,
that the hive was ready to surround it, keep it warm,
feed it nectar, hum to it the most beautiful songs.

They were telling it every kind of lie –
maybe they're not lies if you believe them.

Branchos

When Apollo fell for the shepherd Branchos,
whether the god first kissed the boy, or the boy
the god, scholia disagree and the iambus
of Callimachus has reached us in only
a tattered papyrus. This much we know:
there was an encounter in a wood, a kiss;
Branchos received a garland, a laurel wand,
and skill in prophesy.
And nothing was the same for Branchos after that.

He was set up for life, for one thing,
practicing divination, but it wasn't just the job:
when the god breathed into him, sunlight
pierced the lime-green leaves, birds
called in the branches. With the touch
of the god's lips, a warmth entered him, a sympathy
by which he felt stirrings in the souls
of all who sought his help.
He abandoned his previous life –
there would always be someone to look after sheep.

And was Apollo changed? Did he in later years
remember that tremble in the wood?
He was a god and there were many boys to kiss.

The Poet Ryan

i.m. Gerard Ryan

The old poet in the White House pub:
'I received this letter from Micheál ...'
(of the rice-powdered cheeks).

A tattered papyrus carefully unfolded;
a few words faintly discernible:
'My friend ... Affectionately ...'
Frail and dry as a moth's wing.

A glass of whiskey for the old poet
anointed with the dust of fame.

10 Rue Lepsius

Maybe I should have gone along,
given in to what he wanted,
but he was hesitant, polite, easy to refuse.

My friends had warned me –
You know why he's invited you,
they laughed. I knew, but I was 22
and could look after myself,
and after all he was sort of famous,
a writer, and I was a little flattered.

He offered me a drink. I had just one,
as did he. The flat was shabby,
with no electricity, but didn't look too bad
in the light from oil lamps and candles.

He wanted to know all about me –
the family history, my brothers and sisters,
what I wanted in life. To illustrate a point
he sat beside me on the old sofa
and read something from a book
in a dialect of Greek I didn't understand,
leaning towards me. I leaned away.

And that was it. We finished our drinks,
he thanked me for coming, and said
he had to go out to meet someone,
an editor I think.

I went to the café where my friends were waiting.
They joked a lot and wouldn't believe
nothing had happened. But how could it have?
He's a filthy old man, I said,
and felt myself blushing at having said that.

I saw him again a few weeks later
in a café talking with another young man,
and wanted to go up and say hello,
but felt jealous, and left.

That was twenty years ago. Since then
I've been with lots of women
who weren't as nice as him.

Maybe he would have written something about me;
I could show people the book
and say, See that young man he talks about there –
that was me. But it's too late now;
he's been dead for years.

If I could do it over again? Why fool myself –
it would all be just the same.

Daring Billy

Billy Collins in a poem on Catullus
jokingly calls him 'a foul mouthed cocksucker',
thrilled by the poet's daring obscenities
aimed at his friends,

but if Billy would really honor Catullus
(who had the balls to give Caesar the finger)
he'd insult those pussys and impotent pricks
who made him our poet laureate,

not Catullus who neither can answer back
nor knock him off the short list for a Pultizer.

A THOUGHT WHICH HAD NEVER OCCURRED TO THEM

You can imagine the women's distress,
when they arrived with spices to anoint
the beloved, to discover
the tomb opened and the body gone,

and in its place two beautiful men
who said to them, Why do you seek
the living among the dead? A thought
so obvious it had never occurred to them,

but which now they hurried to report
to the men who had been his friends,
who didn't believe a word of it,
taking it as women's foolishness.

INTO THE DARK MIDWEST CAME THE POET

A chunky silver bracelet
mocked St. Augustine.

A fat gold ring
asked if we'd heard of Garcia Lorca.

A silver bauble quoted
the banalities of an Italian philosopher:

'The coming being is whatever being …'

A tasteful cashmere sweater
assumed the pose of a European intellectual

bringer of light to the dark Midwest
from Twin Falls, Idaho, by way of Vancouver.

WEATHER REPORT

The sun found
and hid behind
the one small cloud
in the whole blue sky.

Portraits in the Gulbenkian Museum, Lisbon

And in this gallery we enter the light
of the eighteenth century.
Scientists look out with confidence.
Upon the scholar's desk, the retort,
astrolabe, and microscope replace
the desiccated skull. Progress now begins.

Happily we leave behind the gaunt ascetics
lost in their unhealthy meditations,
to join the company of rational men
smug beside their quaint scientific instruments.

Heretics

Under the heretics' weights
Margaret Clitherow's ribs
snapped, burst through her side.

Jesu! Jesu! Jesu!
have mercy on me! she cried.
It took a quarter of an hour for her to die.

Master Ridley from the pyre,
too, cried out, Lord
have mercy upon me!

before the flames reached up
and touched the bag of gunpowder
tied around his neck.

That there was cruelty on both sides
is taken by some as proof
that Christianity is a lie.

But perhaps it was not unreasonable
for Nicholas and Margaret both
to cast their hope upon
love crucified.

The Day the World Ended

was an ordinary day in early spring:

people driving to work
kids on their way to school

a morning cool, bright, and clear.

It must have been during the night
that the world had ended

for nobody seemed to have noticed
that time had achieved its fullness

and nothing remained to be done
but to live out our days in peace as best we could.

The world had not ended with trembling and
trumpets:

it was the fact that the ordinary continued
that signaled the world's completion –

people driving to work
kids on their way to school

as if it was an ordinary day in early spring.

O Heart

At Mass
she holds
an old
magnifying glass
over the
worn pages
of her
prayerbook.
Kneeling
behind her
I see
two words
fill up
that lens:
Sweet Jesus.
O heart
of mine
be like
that glass.

Every Time

The sidewalks were covered with packed snow
glazed with ice as he came down the front steps
on his walker. 'The sidewalk's very bad today',
I said. 'You used to see me with my dog',
he said. 'She took a walk with me every day.
We had to put her down. She was shaking
and the vet said she had cancer. My doctor says
I shouldn't have a dog; she'd get under my feet
and I'd fall. I miss her'. The old man.
His gentle voice. He said this every time we met.

REMEMBER

Remember the rules you learned in childhood –
how to present yourself, how to behave?
Politeness. Propriety.
Forget all that.

And growing up – neatness, cleanliness, punctuality,
a job well done.
Forget that, too.

And later, learning to accept both your own
inadequacies
and the failings of others – remember how much
peace that brought you?
Forget all that.

Remember how your mother used to wash your hair.

Remember the beloved's smile, lying back,
the first time, moonlight pouring over both of you.

Remember at the *Agnus Dei* mercy flooding the
cathedral.

Remember that.

The Waterfall

I too hold my small cup
under the waterfall.

About the Author

Jim Chapson, born in Honolulu, Hawaii, in 1944, was educated at San Francisco State University, and now teaches satire and other forms of writing at the University of Wisconsin-Milwaukee. He has had chapbooks published by White Rabbit, hit & run, and Blue Canary presses. This is his first book-length collection.

ACKNOWLEDGEMENTS

Grateful acknowledgment is made to the editors of the following periodicals in which some of these poems first appeared: *Poetry Ireland Review, The Blue Canary, The SHOp, Prairie Spooner, Burdock, B-Squad, Rust Buckle, The Saturday Evening Bath, Donkey Jaw,* and *The New England Journal of Buggery.*

For translations from Theocritus and Callimachus, acknowledgement is made to Robert Wells, *The Idylls of Theocritus* (Carcanet, 1988); and Frank Nisetich, *The Poems of Callimachus* (Oxford, 2001).